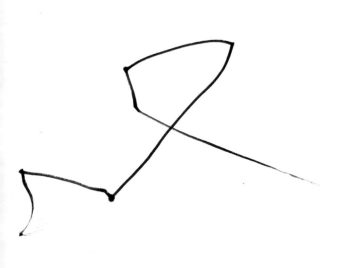

Guy the Shy Fly

Jan Westberg

Consulting Editor, Diane Craig, M.A./Reading Specialist

ABDO
Publishing Company

Published by ABDO Publishing Company, 4940 Viking Drive, Edina, Minnesota 55435.

Printed in the United States.

Credits
Edited by: Pam Price
Curriculum Coordinator: Nancy Tuminelly
Cover and Interior Design and Production: Mighty Media
Photo and Illustration Credits: Brand X Pictures, Comstock, Corbis Images, Eyewire Images, Hemera, Image Source, Tracy Kompelien

Library of Congress Cataloging-in-Publication Data

Westberg, Jan.
     Guy the shy fly / Jan Westberg.
        p. cm. -- (Rhyme time)
     Includes index.
     ISBN 1-59197-793-2 (hardcover)
     ISBN 1-59197-899-8 (paperback)
     1. English language--Rhyme--Juvenile literature. I. Title. II. Rhyme time (ABDO Publishing Company)

     PE1517.W4775 2004
     808.1--dc22
                                                                          2004049043

SandCastle™ books are created by a professional team of educators, reading specialists, and content developers around five essential components that include phonemic awareness, phonics, vocabulary, text comprehension, and fluency. All books are written, reviewed, and leveled for guided reading, early intervention reading, and Accelerated Reader® programs and designed for use in shared, guided, and independent reading and writing activities to support a balanced approach to literacy instruction.

Let Us Know

After reading the book, SandCastle would like you to tell us your stories about reading. What is your favorite page? Was there something hard that you needed help with? Share the ups and downs of learning to read. We want to hear from you! To get posted on the ABDO Publishing Company Web site, send us e-mail at:

sandcastle@abdopub.com

SandCastle Level: Transitional

Words that rhyme do not have to be spelled the same. These words rhyme with each other:

buy

fly

cry

guy

dry

my

dye

rye

eye

shy

Tracy's mom holds her so she won't **cry** any more.

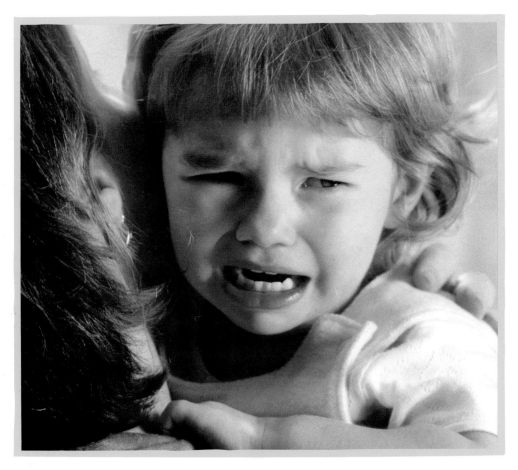

Marcy and her mom went to the store to buy new shoes.

After Abe washes his dad's car,
he will wipe it **dry**.

Johanna's mom dips an egg into the green **dye**.

Sometimes T.J. pretends to fly.

Ruth is playing peekaboo with her dad.

They each cover one **eye**.

When Derek gave his mom
a birthday gift, she exclaimed,
"Oh my!"

When Quentin shares his treat with his sister, he feels like a nice **guy**.

When Susan has a question, she is not too **shy** to ask her teacher.

For lunch, Leo has a sandwich on white bread, not rye.

Guy the Shy Fly

Guy was a fly
who was very shy.

Sometimes Guy would cry
without knowing why.

It's a funny thing to see a fly
with a tear in its eye.

Guy sure did love to fly.
He flew over many foods
he wanted to try.

One day he flew very high
over a large loaf of raisin rye.

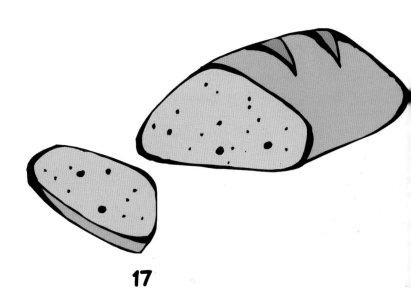

That evening he did spy
a great big bowl of purple dye.

Guy thought to himself,
"I'll give that a try."

He dove into the bowl and gave a sigh.
Then he flew around until he was dry.

As Guy went past a mirror,
he said, "Oh my!

I'll be purple until next July!"

Just as Guy was about to cry,
his best friend, Ty, came flying by.

Ty said, "That color you can't deny.
It's about time you stopped being shy!"

What do you call
stale dark bread?

Dry rye

Glossary

deny. to refuse to believe, admit, acknowledge, or permit something

dye. a liquid that is used to change the color of something

exclaim. to speak loudly and with strong feeling

rye. a cereal grass grown for its grain; dark bread made from rye flour

shy. timid, bashful, or uncomfortable around others

About SandCastle™

A professional team of educators, reading specialists, and content developers created the SandCastle™ series to support young readers as they develop reading skills and strategies and increase their general knowledge. The SandCastle™ series has four levels that correspond to early literacy development in young children. The levels are provided to help teachers and parents select the appropriate books for young readers.

Emerging Readers
(no flags)

Beginning Readers
(1 flag)

Transitional Readers
(2 flags)

Fluent Readers
(3 flags)

These levels are meant only as a guide. All levels are subject to change.

To see a complete list of SandCastle™ books and other nonfiction titles from ABDO Publishing Company, visit www.abdopub.com or contact us at:
4940 Viking Drive, Edina, Minnesota 55435 • 1-800-800-1312 • fax: 1-952-831-1632